W9-CTX-150

1

SECOND EDITION

STEP FORWARD

STANDARDS-BASED LANGUAGE LEARNING
FOR WORK AND ACADEMIC READINESS

SERIES DIRECTOR
Jayme Adelson-Goldstein

Workbook

THIS BOOK IS THE PROPERTY OF
THE NATIONAL CITY PUBLIC LIBRARY
1401 NATIONAL CITY BLVD
NATIONAL CITY, CA 91950

REFERENCE USE ONLY
NOT TO BE TAKEN
FROM LIBRARY

Janet Podnecky

OXFORD
UNIVERSITY PRESS

OXFORD
UNIVERSITY PRESS

198 Madison Avenue
New York, NY 10016 USA

Great Clarendon Street, Oxford, OX2 6DP, United Kingdom

Oxford University Press is a department of the University of Oxford.
It furthers the University's objective of excellence in research, scholarship,
and education by publishing worldwide. Oxford is a registered trade
mark of Oxford University Press in the UK and in certain other countries

© Oxford University Press 2017

The moral rights of the author have been asserted

First published in 2017

2021 2020 2019 2018 2017

10 9 8 7 6 5 4 3 2 1

No unauthorized photocopying

All rights reserved. No part of this publication may be reproduced, stored
in a retrieval system, or transmitted, in any form or by any means, without
the prior permission in writing of Oxford University Press, or as expressly
permitted by law, by licence or under terms agreed with the appropriate
reprographics rights organization. Enquiries concerning reproduction outside
the scope of the above should be sent to the ELT Rights Department, Oxford
University Press, at the address above

You must not circulate this work in any other form and you must impose
this same condition on any acquirer

Links to third party websites are provided by Oxford in good faith and for
information only. Oxford disclaims any responsibility for the materials
contained in any third party website referenced in this work

ISBN: 978 0 19 449323 9 (WORKBOOK LEVEL 1)

Printed in China

This book is printed on paper from certified and well-managed sources

ACKNOWLEDGMENTS

Illustrations by: Susan Spellman: pp. 2, 5, 11, 16, 24, 39, 57, 61, 65; Richard
Deverell: pp. 6, 18, 31, 33, 51, 55, 73; Kevin Brown: pp. 24, 25, 29, 35, 40, 41, 47,
52, 59, 63, 74, 76, 84, 86, 87, 88; Kathy Baxendale: pp. 2, 9, 23, 30, 41, 44, 72,
78, 79; Rose Lowry: 2(tl), 39(r); Gary Torrisi: 7, 13, 26, 37, 46, 58, 68, 82; Karen
Minot: pp. 10, 17, 19, 20, 34, 44, 45, 70, 80.

*The publishers would like to thank the following for their kind permission to reproduce
photographs*: Cover, Click Bestsellers / Shutterstock.com; pg. 4 Monkey Business
Images/Shutterstock; pg. 10 Digital Media Pro/Shutterstock; pg. 16 Klaus
Tiedge/Blend Images/GettyImages; pg. 17 Blend Images/Superstock, Manchan/
Digitalvision/Getty Images; pg. 19 Erik Reis/Alamy, iko/Shutterstock; pg. 23
Abode/Corbis/Getty Images, Andy Dean Photography/Alamy, Design Pics Inc/
Alamy, Blend Images - BUILT Content/Alamy; pg. 27 uchenik/Shutterstock;
pg. 28 David J. Green - Lifestyle/Alamy; pg. 32 Rostislav Glinsky/Shutterstock;
pg. 38 Levent Konuk/Shutterstock; pg. 42 Ariel Skelley/Blend Images/Getty
Images; pg. 49 Yukmin/Asia Images/Getty Images; pg. 65 Marc Romanelli/
Blend Images/Getty Images, Lane Oatey/Blue Jean Images/Getty Images; pg. 66
Jeff Greenberg/Contributor/Universal Images Group/Getty Images; pg. 67
Antonio Guillem/Shutterstock; pg. 72 FocusDzign/Shutterstock; pg. 80 Glow
Images/Superstock; pg. 81 Barry Lewis/Alamy.

CONTENTS

A Match the words with the pictures.

| ____ say | ____ sit down | ____ close | ____ open |
| 1 listen to | ____ point to | ____ stand up | ____ repeat |

B Read the words. Look around the classroom. Circle the singular and plural words for the things and people you see.

1. a chair / (chairs)
2. (a teacher) / teachers
3. a student / students
4. a desk / desks
5. a book / books
6. a pen / pens
7. a clock / clocks
8. a board / boards

A Read the form.

School Registration Form

Name: _____Martinez_____Elena_____
         (last)   (first)

Address: _118 Linden Street, Apt. 18, Andover, MA 21156_
          (street)   (city/state)   (zip code)

Telephone: _(617) 555-1345_____
            (area code)

Email: ___emartinez@work.us_____

Signature: ___Elena Martinez_____

B Look at the form in A. Circle *a* or *b*.

1. Tell me your first name.
   a. Martinez
   (b.) Elena

2. Tell me your telephone number.
   a. (617) 555-1345
   b. 21156

3. Write your email address.
   a. emartinez@work.us
   b. 118 Linden Street

4. Please spell your last name.
   a. M-A-R-T-I-N-E-Z
   b. E-L-E-N-A

5. Please write your address.
   a. Elena Martinez
   b. 118 Linden Street, Apt. 18

6. Please sign your name.
   a. Elena Martinez
   b. *Elena Martinez*

C Complete the form. Use your own information. Sign your name.

School Registration Form

Name: _____
         (last)   (first)

Address: _____
          (street)   (city/state)   (zip code)

Telephone: _____
            (area code)

Email: _____

Signature: _____

A **Circle the correct words.**

1. He (is / are) a student.
2. We (are / is) in class.
3. I (am / is) not a teacher.
4. They (is / are) my classmates.
5. You (are / am) in my group.
6. It (am / is) my book.
7. Mr. Sims (is / are) my teacher.
8. She (is / are) my friend.

B **Complete the sentences. Use *am, is,* or *are*.**

1. He _____is_____ my partner.
2. We _____ in the classroom.
3. You _____ a teacher.
4. They _____ in my group.
5. I _____ at my desk.
6. It _____ my dictionary.
7. She _____ a student.
8. Elena and Dan _____ teachers.

C **Rewrite the sentences in B. Make them negative.**

1. He is not my partner. _____
2. _____
3. _____
4. _____
5. _____
6. _____
7. _____
8. _____

D Rewrite the sentences. Use contractions for the underlined words.

1. <u>I am</u> a student.　　　　I'm a student. _____

2. We <u>are not</u> teachers.　　_____

3. The teacher <u>is not</u> here.　_____

4. She <u>is not</u> in the classroom.　_____

5. <u>You are</u> my partner.　　_____

6. <u>They are</u> listening.　　_____

7. <u>I am</u> not at school.　　_____

8. <u>He is</u> a teacher.　　　_____

E Unscramble the sentences.

1. am / in / not / I / the classroom

   I am not in the classroom. _____

2. not / students / They / are

   _____

3. classmate / You / my / are

   _____

4. We / in / school / are

   _____

5. my / is / It / book

   _____

6. teacher / not / is / She / my

   _____

A Complete the conversation. Use the words in the box.

you later	And you	~~Good morning~~	Fine	How are

Ana: Good morning, Mr. Han.

Mr. Han: _Good morning_ , Ana.

      1

Ana: _____ you?

     2

Mr. Han: Fine, thanks. _____?

         3

Ana: _____. See _____, Mr. Han.

     4   5

Mr. Han: Goodbye, Ana.

B Complete the conversation. Use your own information.

1. **A:** Hi, I'm Nadel. What's your name?

   B: _____

2. **A:** Can you repeat that, please?

   B: _____

3. **A:** How are you?

   B: _____

4. **A:** It's nice to meet you.

   B: _____

5. **A:** Goodbye.

   B: _____

DO THE MATH Go to page 86.

A Look at the pictures. Write the correct words under each picture. Use the words in the box.

~~study~~ go to school listen to the radio ask for help

1. _____study_____ 2. _____ 3. _____ 4. _____

B Look at the chart. Match the numbers with the information.

How Students in Class 2B Study English

Hi, I'm Hassan. I'm a student in Class 2B. This is how the students in my class study English.

Study Methods	Number of Adults
speak English at home	6
read in English	4
listen to the radio	12
study at home	3

How many students...

_d_ 1. read in English?   a. 3 students

____ 2. study at home?   b. 6 students

____ 3. listen to the radio?   c. 12 students

____ 4. speak English at home?   d. 4 students

C How do you learn English? Check (✔) your study method(s).

____ read in English   ____ listen to the radio

____ study at home   ____ speak English at home

A Complete the questions and the instructions. Use the code.

1=a	2=b	3=c	4=d	5=e	6=f
7=g	8=h	9=i	10=j	11=k	12=l
13=m	14=n	15=o	16=p	17=q	18=r
19=s	20=t	21=u	22=v	23=w	24=x
25=y	26=z				

1. W h a t ' s your f i r s t n a m e ?
   23 8 1 20 19   6 9 18 19 20 14 1 13 5

2. How _ _ _ _ _ _ ?
   1 18 5   25 15 21

3. _ _ _ _ _ _ _ your _ _ _ _ _ _ _ _ _ .
   20 5 12 12   13 5   1 4 4 18 5 19 19

4. _ _ _ _ _ _ ' _ _ _ _ _ _ _ _ _ _ number?
   23 8 1 20 19   25 15 21 18   16 8 15 14 5

5. _ _ _ _ _ _ your _ _ _ _ _ _ .
   19 9 7 14   14 1 13 5

B Look at A. Answer the questions and follow the instructions. Use complete sentences and your own information.

What's your first name? My first name is...

1. _____

2. _____

3. _____

4. _____

5. _____

A Look at the clocks. Write the times two ways.

1. <u>5:00</u>   2. _____   3. _____

   <u>five o'clock</u>   _____   _____

4. _____   5. _____   6. _____

   _____   _____   _____

B Complete the chart. Use the words in the box.

| ~~Monday~~ 11/20/1998   Friday   ~~5:45~~   4:30   March |
| October   January   3/16/17   7/18/2020 Thursday   2:00 |

Time	Day	Month	Date
5:45	Monday		

A Read the form.

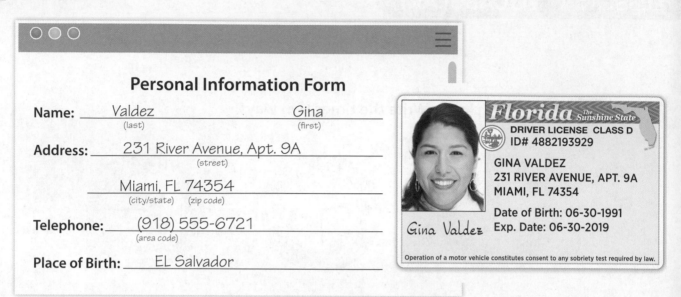

B Look at the form in A. Complete the sentences.

1. My _____name_____ is Gina Valdez.

2. I'm from _____.

3. My _____ of birth is June 30, 1991.

4. My _____ number is (918) 555-6721.

5. I _____ in Miami, FL.

6. My _____ is 231 River Avenue, Apt. 9A.

C Answer the questions. Use complete sentences and your own information.

1. What's your name?

_____

2. Where are you from?

_____

3. What's your date of birth?

_____

4. Where do you live?

_____

5. What's your address?

_____

6. What's your telephone number?

_____

A Look at the pictures. Write the correct words under the pictures. Use the words in the box.

| tired | happy | angry | ~~worried~~ | hungry | proud |

1. _____worried_____   3. _____   5. _____

2. _____   4. _____   6. _____

B Match the questions with the answers.

_c_ 1. Are you angry?   a. Yes, they are.

____ 2. Is Paul tired?   b. It's black.

____ 3. Is Sophie worried or sad?   c. No, I'm not.

____ 4. Are the students happy?   d. Yes, he is.

____ 5. Is your phone black or white?   e. She's worried.

C Read the sentences. Then write *yes/no* questions. Use the words in parentheses.

1. Sara is from New York. (Mark)

   Is Mark from New York?

2. Nadel and Tom are proud. (Lilia)

   _____

3. Anh is from Vietnam. (Carol and Pam)

   _____

4. We are tired. (Daniel)

   _____

5. I am hungry. (you)

   _____

D Read the answers. Write the *yes/no* questions. Use the words in parentheses.

1. (you / sad)

   A: _Are you sad?_

   B: Yes, I am.

2. (the students / tired)

   A: _____

   B: No, they aren't.

3. (Juan / from Mexico)

   A: _____

   B: No, he isn't.

4. (the teacher / in the classroom)

   A: _____

   B: Yes, she is.

5. (this workbook / yellow)

   A: _____

   B: Yes, it is.

6. (we / happy)

   A: _____

   B: No, we aren't.

E Unscramble the questions. Then match the questions with the answers.

___c___ 1. name / your / What / is

       What is your name?

_____ 2. from / you / Where / are

      _____

_____ 3. your / What / is / date of birth

      _____

_____ 4. he / a student / Is / or / a teacher

      _____

a. I'm from Haiti.

b. He's a student.

c. My name is Eric.

d. My date of birth is 6/10/90.

A **Read the form.**

Appointment Time: 3:30 p.m.

Name: ___Peng___ ___Yoshi___
         (last)   (first)

Address: ___3933 Ross Avenue, San Jose, CA 95124___
         (street)   (city/state)   (zip code)

Telephone: ___(209) 555-7455___
         (area code)

Date of Birth: ___5/6/1986___

Place of Birth: ___Japan___

Marital Status: (married) single

PATIENT SIGN IN

B **You are Yoshi Peng in A. Answer the questions. Use complete sentences.**

1. What's your last name?

   My last name is Peng.

2. What's your first name?

   _____

3. Are you married or single?

   _____

4. What's your address?

   _____

5. What's your date of birth?

   _____

6. Where are you from?

   _____

C **Answer the questions. Use your own information.**

1. What's your last name?

   _____

2. Are you married or single?

   _____

3. Where are you from?

   _____

4. What's your date of birth?

   _____

DO THE MATH Go to page 87.

LESSON 5 READING

A Complete the sentences. Use the words in the box.

| population statehood ~~million~~ |

1. 1,000,000 is one ___million___.
2. The date of _____ is the date of birth for a state.
3. The _____ of the United States is 325 million people.

B Read the article. Where is California?

California: An Interesting State

California is a state in the United States. It's date of statehood is September 9, 1850. Today, the population of California is about 39 million people. 15.1 million are Latin American. 5.4 million are Asian. Ten million are from other countries. Six million are students.

C Look at the article in B. Circle *a* or *b*.

1. California is a _____.
   a. state
   b. country

2. What is California's date of statehood?
   a. the United States
   b. September 9, 1850

3. What is the population of California?
   a. 39 million people
   b. 5.4 million people

4. Are 15.1 million Latin Americans in California?
   a. Yes
   b. No

5. Are ten or six million people students in California?
   a. ten
   b. six

A Look at the chart. Cross out (X) the example word that does not belong in each line.

Category	Examples
Days	Tuesday Saturday ~~March~~ Monday
Months	January Sunday June October
Dates	3/16/1952 7/18/17 12:10 11/20/2014
Times	9:30 1990 10:15 4 p.m.
Colors	red blue yellow month
Feelings	happy today worried hungry
Countries	China April Russia Mexico
Continents	Street Africa South America Europe

B Write sentences. Use a word from each category.

(Days) <u>Today is Wednesday.</u>   (Continents) <u>Sam is from Africa.</u>

1. (Days) _____

2. (Months) _____

3. (Dates) _____

4. (Times) _____

5. (Colors) _____

6. (Feelings) _____

7. (Countries) _____

8. (Continents) _____

A Who is in your family? Check (✔) the words.

____ husband	____ brother	____ mother-in-law
____ wife	____ sister	____ father-in-law
____ father	____ aunt	____ sister-in-law
____ mother	____ uncle	____ brother-in-law
____ son	____ grandfather	____ son-in-law
____ daughter	____ grandmother	____ daughter-in-law
____ children	____ cousin	

B Look at Christine and her family. Complete the sentences.

Grandparents

John   Amy

Father   Mother

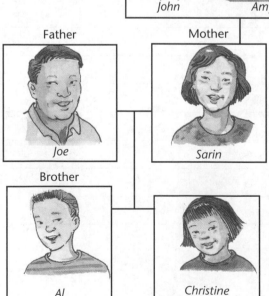

Joe   Sarin

Brother

Al   Christine

1. Sarin is the ____mother____.

2. _____ is the brother.

3. Joe is the _____.

4. John and _____
   are the _____.

A Look at the ID cards. Complete the sentences.

My ____name____ is Marie.
     1
_____ _____ are brown.
    2   3
My _____ _____ black.
       4   5

CALIFORNIA   IDENTIFICATION CARD

Marie Santos
ID# 673-9295011

Eye Color: brown
Hair Color: black
Date of Birth: 03/25/1996

Marie Santos

My name is _____.
                6
My eyes _____ _____.
           7   8
_____ _____ is blond.
    9   10

CALIFORNIA   IDENTIFICATION CARD

Pavel Turek
ID# 842-1314772

Eye Color: blue
Hair Color: blond
Date of Birth: 06/11/1994

Pavel Turek

B Answer the questions. Use complete sentences and your own information.

What is your name? My name is David.

1. What is your name?

   _____

2. What color are your eyes?

   _____

3. What color is your hair?

   _____

4. Are you tall or short?

   _____

C Write a paragraph about yourself. Use the information in B.

What is your name? My name is David.

My name is _____. My eyes _____ _____.

_____ _____ _____ _____.

_____ _____ _____.

A Circle the correct words.

1. Hi. (My / Your) name is Ines.

2. This is Ron. (Their / His) brother is in this class.

3. We are in the class. (Her / Our) teacher is Mr. Flynn.

4. Rita is in class. (Her / His) papers are on the table.

5. Where are the students? (Their / Her) books are here.

6. This is for you. It's (their / your) book.

B Match the questions with the answers.

_d_ 1. Is your sister tall?	a.	Yes, they are brown.
____ 2. Are your eyes blue?	b.	Yes, she is here.
____ 3. Is Mark's hair blond?	c.	Yes, I'm their friend.
____ 4. Are Karen's eyes brown?	d.	Yes, she is tall.
____ 5. Is my sister in class today?	e.	No, his hair is brown.
____ 6. Are you Sam and Tom's friend?	f.	No, my eyes are green.

C Complete the sentences. Use possessive adjectives that match the underlined words.

1. I like _____my_____ family and friends.

2. Sasha is a good friend. She has a big family. _____ family is nice.

3. Olga is in school. _____ family is from Russia.

4. David and Tony are not in this class, but _____ sister is.

5. We like the class and _____ teacher.

6. Are you a new student? What's _____ name?

7. The school is good. _____ name is South Street Training Center.

8. Are you and Paul ready? Where are _____ books?

D Look at the ID cards. Write four sentences about each person. Use possessive adjectives and the words in parentheses.

1. (name) <u>His name is Paul Allen.</u>
2. (eyes) _____
3. (hair) _____
4. (date of birth) _____

5. (name) _____
6. (eyes) _____
7. (hair) _____
8. (date of birth) _____

E Complete the questions with *Paul's* or *Sasha's*. Then complete the answers with *his* or *her*.

1. **A:** What is ____Paul's____ last name?

   B: <u>His</u> _____ last name is Allen.

2. **A:** What color are _____ eyes?

   B: _____ eyes are blue.

3. **A:** What is _____ last name?

   B: _____ last name is Tomlin.

4. **A:** What color is _____ hair?

   B: _____ hair is blond.

5. **A:** What color is _____ hair?

   B: _____ hair is black.

6. **A:** What is _____ date of birth?

   B: _____ date of birth is 01/12/1992.

7. **A:** What color are _____ eyes?

   B: _____ eyes are green.

8. **A:** What is _____ ID #?

   B: _____ ID# is 973-9265021.

A **Complete the conversation. Use the words in the box.**

the date today	~~day is today~~	birthday
October 10th	that's right	It's Tuesday

David: Hi, Marie. What _____ day is today _____?
1

Marie: _____.
2

David: What's _____?
3

Marie: It's _____.
4

David: Tuesday, October 10th?

Marie: Yes, _____.
5

David: Oh, no. Today is Tom's _____.
6

B **Write the dates.**

1. 3/16 _March 16th_   3. 2/22 _____   5. 11/20 _____

2. 6/21 _____   4. 8/9 _____   6. 7/31 _____

C **Look at the calendar. Answer the questions. Use complete sentences.**

1. What day is today? _Today is Friday._ _____

2. What is the date? _____

3. When is Marie's birthday? _____

4. What day is June 9th? _____

DO THE MATH Go to page 88.

A **Look at the graph. Read the article. Are all families the same?**

Families in the United States

In the United States, families are large and small. There are families with many children. There are families with no children. In many families, there is a married couple[1] at home. In other families, there is only an adult male[2] at home. In other families, there is only an adult female[3] at home.

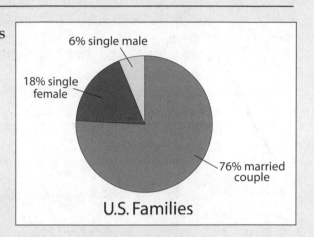

6% single male

18% single female

76% married couple

U.S. Families

[1]couple = two people
[2]male = man
[3]female = woman

B **Look at the article and graph in A. Circle *a* or *b*.**

1. In the United States, families are large and _____.
   a. married
   (b.) small

2. In eighteen percent of families, there is _____.
   a. only an adult woman
   b. only an adult male

3. In seventy-six percent of families, there is _____.
   a. many children
   b. a married couple

4. In _____ of families, there is only an adult man at home.
   a. eighteen percent
   b. six percent

A Unscramble the words.

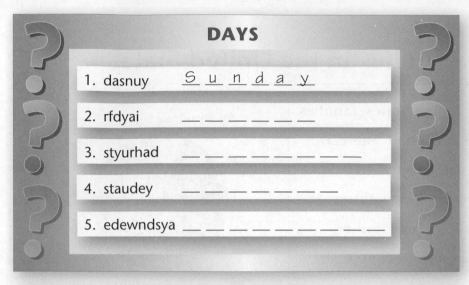

DAYS

1. dasnuy   <u>S u n d a y</u>
2. rfdyai   _ _ _ _ _ _
3. styurhad   _ _ _ _ _ _ _ _
4. staudey   _ _ _ _ _ _ _
5. edewndsya _ _ _ _ _ _ _ _ _

MONTHS

1. utagus   _ _ _ _ _ _
2. nayjura   _ _ _ _ _ _ _
3. perstbmee _ _ _ _ _ _ _ _ _
4. tobreco   _ _ _ _ _ _ _
5. onebervm _ _ _ _ _ _ _ _

B Complete the words in each sentence with one letter. Use the letters in the box.

a	e	i	o	u

1. Sue's h_<u>a</u>_ir is bl_<u>a</u>_ck.
2. Th___s ___s my s___ster-___n-law Sue.
3. H___r ___y___s ar___ gr_____n.
4. My ___unt is t___ll ___nd be___utiful.
5. O___r ___ncle has bl___e eyes.
6. Y___ur c___usin's hair is br___wn.

LESSON 1 VOCABULARY

A Match the words with the pictures.

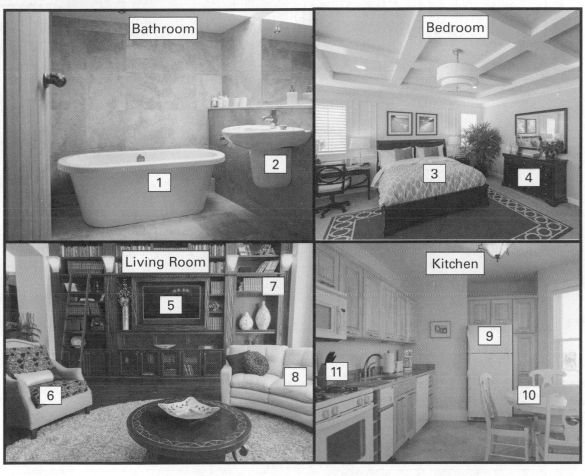

____ bed   ____ sofa   ____ refrigerator   ____ TV

____ table   _1_ bathtub   ____ stove   ____ bookcase

____ sink   ____ dresser   ____ chair

B Look at the pictures in A. Answer the questions. Use complete sentences.

1. Where's the sofa? _The sofa is in the living room._____

2. Where's the stove? _____

3. Is the bed in the kitchen? _____

4. Is the bathtub in the bedroom? _____

A **Look at the picture. Complete the chart. Use the words in the box.**

yard	washing the car	sleeping
kitchen	playing games	~~bedroom~~

Who?	Where?	What?
1. Clara	_bedroom_	_____
2. Mr. Vegas	_____	cooking dinner
3. David and Linda	living room	_____
4. Mrs. Vegas	_____	listening to music
5. Luis	outside	_____

B **Complete the sentences. Use the words in the chart in A.**

It's a beautiful day. Mrs. Vegas is _____listening to music_____. She's in the

_____. Mr. Vegas is in the _____. He's
     2   3

_____. Clara is sleeping. She's in the _____.
     4   5

David and Linda are _____ in the _____. Luis
                            6   7

is outside. He's _____. It's a great day to do some work or relax.
                       8

LESSON **3** GRAMMAR

A Circle the correct words.

1. Hi. My name is Ellen. (**I** / He) am cleaning the kitchen.

2. This is my roommate, Claire. (She / We) is studying.

3. (We / I) are cooking dinner.

4. (He / You) are sitting in my chair.

5. These are our friends. (He / They) are playing in the yard.

6. Now, (you / I) am listening to music.

B Complete the sentences. Use the present continuous and the verbs in parentheses.

1. We _____are watching_____ a video right now. (watch)

2. Our teacher _____ some work. (do)

3. I _____ an email. (read)

4. Javier and Eduardo _____ in the kitchen. (eat)

5. Patty _____ in the bedroom. (sleep)

6. The teacher _____ to the students. (listen)

C Write sentences. Use the present continuous.

1. We / clean / the house / today

   We are cleaning the house today.

2. My / brother / mop / the kitchen

   _____

3. Our / friends / wash / the car

   _____

4. My / mother / open / the refrigerator

   _____

5. Our / cousin / wash / the dishes

   _____

6. I / watch / TV

   _____

D Look at the pictures. Write information questions. Then write the answers. Use the present continuous.

Laura

1. What is Laura doing?

   She's studying.

Patty and Rose

2. _____

   _____

David and Maritza

3. _____

   _____

Pete

4. _____

   _____

E Add *-ing*. Rewrite the verbs.

1. play   →   _____playing_____

2. mop   →   _____

3. do   →   _____

4. give   →   _____

5. close   →   _____

6. stop   →   _____

A Read the bills.

💡 **Central State Electric Co.**	📱 **CellTele Phone Co.**	💧 **Hydro Clear**
Amount due: $52.50	Amount due: $88.00	*Amount due:* $25.00
due date 5/12/18	due date 5/23/18	due date 5/27/18

B Complete the conversation. Use the words in the box.

May 12th	the electric bill	~~are you~~
I help you	the due date	paying

Minh: What _____are you_____ doing?
                              1

John: I'm _____ the bills.
                              2

Minh: Can _____?
                        3

John: Yes, please. Where's _____?
                                              4

Minh: Here it is.

John: What's _____?
                              5

Minh: It's _____.
                        6

John: Oh, that's tomorrow! I'm paying that bill today!

C Unscramble the sentences. Then write *P* for problem or *S* for suggestion.

_P_ 1. a / There's / problem

    There's a problem.

____ 2. fix / it / Let's

____ 3. isn't / working / It

____ 4. manual / at / look / Let's / the

____ 5. this / Try

____ 6. broken / It's

A Read the tips. How is Tara saving money?

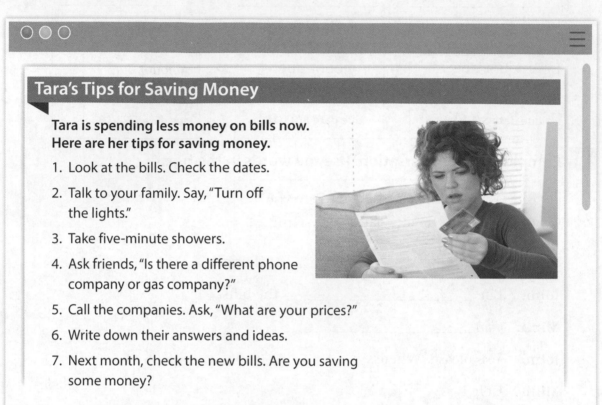

Tara's Tips for Saving Money

Tara is spending less money on bills now. Here are her tips for saving money.

1. Look at the bills. Check the dates.

2. Talk to your family. Say, "Turn off the lights."

3. Take five-minute showers.

4. Ask friends, "Is there a different phone company or gas company?"

5. Call the companies. Ask, "What are your prices?"

6. Write down their answers and ideas.

7. Next month, check the new bills. Are you saving some money?

B Read the sentences. Check (✔) the ideas in the article. Mark (X) the ideas NOT in the article.

___✓___ 1. These tips help you save money.

_____ 2. Check the dates on the bills.

_____ 3. Your family helps save on the utilities.

_____ 4. All companies have the same prices.

_____ 5. Ask friends about different companies.

_____ 6. Don't use a cell phone.

A Complete the sentences. Use the words in the box.

mopping	~~bills~~	phone	paying	electric
eating	bedroom	cleaning	stove	

1. I pay the utility _____bills_____ every month.

2. It's Saturday. We're _____ all the rooms in the house.

3. Paul is cooking on the _____ in the kitchen.

4. Please pay the telephone, gas, water, and _____ bills tomorrow.

5. I am _____ the floor.

6. Kara is sleeping in the _____.

7. I'm talking on the _____.

8. We are _____ dinner now.

9. Are you _____ the bills today?

B Complete the puzzle. Use the words in A.

1. b i l l (s)
2. ___ ___ ___ (○) ___ ___ ___
3. ___ ___ (○) ___
4. ___ (○) ___ ___ ___
5. (○) ___ ___ ___ ___ ___
6. ___ ___ ___ ___ (○) ___ ___
7. ___ ___ ___ (○) ___
8. (○) ___ ___ ___ ___
9. ___ ___ (○) ___ ___

C Write the circled letters from the puzzle in B. What's the secret message?

___ ___ ___ ___   ___ ___ ___ ___ ___ !
1 2 3 4   5 6 7 8 9

A Look at the map. Match the words with the picture.

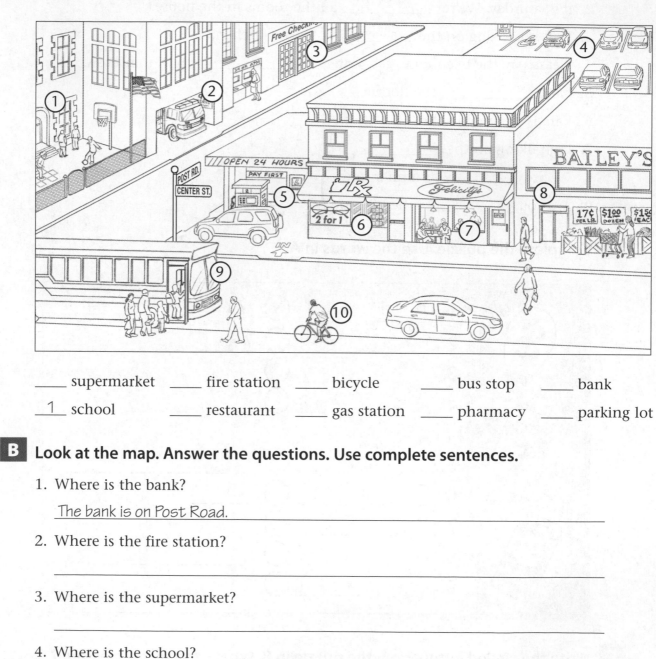

____ supermarket   ____ fire station   ____ bicycle   ____ bus stop   ____ bank

_1_ school   ____ restaurant   ____ gas station   ____ pharmacy   ____ parking lot

B Look at the map. Answer the questions. Use complete sentences.

1. Where is the bank?

   The bank is on Post Road.

2. Where is the fire station?

   _____

3. Where is the supermarket?

   _____

4. Where is the school?

   _____

LESSON 2 WRITING

A Look at the picture. Match the places with the locations.

___b___ 1. The apartment building is

_____ 2. The bank is

_____ 3. The post office is

_____ 4. The pharmacy is

a. across from the apartment building.

b. next to the bank.

c. between the supermarket and the apartment building.

d. across from the bank.

B Look at the picture in A. Complete the paragraph. Use the words in the box.

~~neighborhood~~	an apartment	next to the
a bank	across from my	I live

Let me tell you about my _____neighborhood_____. It's a nice place to live.
                                    1
_____ on River Street. I live in _____.
            2   3
The address is 2919 River Street. There is a post office _____
                                                                      4
apartment building. There is a pharmacy _____ post office.
                                                        5
There is _____ between my apartment and the supermarket.
              6

A **Complete the sentences. Use *There is* or *There are*.**

Southside Mall is a great place for shoppers!

1. <u>There are</u> over 50 stores in the mall.

2. _____ not a convenience store.

3. _____ three banks in the mall.

4. _____ a large parking lot.

5. _____ two movie theaters.

6. _____ eight restaurants.

7. _____ not a supermarket.

8. _____ two pharmacies.

B **Write sentences. Use *There is* and *There are*.**

1. There / many great places / in / my neighborhood

   <u>There are many great places in my neighborhood.</u>

2. There / a movie theater / across from / my home

   _____

3. There / some restaurants / next to / the school

   _____

4. There / a parking lot / behind / the school

   _____

5. There / an apartment building / between / the school / and / the park

   _____

6. There / a bus stop / in front of / the movie theater

   _____

7. There / a mailbox / next to / the park

   _____

8. There / a hospital / behind / the supermarket

   _____

C Look at the picture. Complete the questions. Use *Is there* or *Are there*. Then answer the questions.

1. A: <u>Is there</u> a boy on a bicycle?

   B: <u>Yes, there is.</u>

2. A: _____ a fire fighter in the park?

   B: _____

3. A: _____ an ambulance in the park?

   B: _____

4. A: _____ restaurants in the park?

   B: _____

5. A: _____ children in the park?

   B: _____

6. A: _____ a bus stop near the park?

   B: _____

D Write about your neighborhood. Complete the questions. Use *Is there* or *Are there*. Then write your answers. If you say *yes*, give the location.

Is there a library in your neighborhood?
Yes, there is. It's next to the pharmacy.

1. A: _____ a library in your neighborhood?

   B: _____

2. A: _____ a fire station?

   B: _____

3. A: _____ restaurants?

   B: _____

4. A: _____ banks?

   B: _____

A Look at the map. Complete the conversation. Use the words in the box.

between	blocks	~~Excuse~~	left	right	straight	there	turn

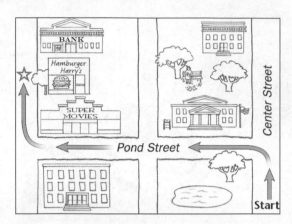

A: <u>Excuse</u> me. Is _____ a restaurant near here?
        1   2

B: Yes, there is. Go _____ on Center Street. Turn _____ on Pond
                                  3   4

Street. Go two _____ on Pond Street. Then _____ right.
                           5   6

The restaurant is on the _____. It's _____ the bank and the
                                         7   8

movie theater.

B Look at the map. Complete the conversation. Give directions from the
bus stop.

A: Excuse me. Is there a bank near here?

B: Yes, there is.

_____

_____

_____

_____

_____

A: Thanks for your help.

B: _____

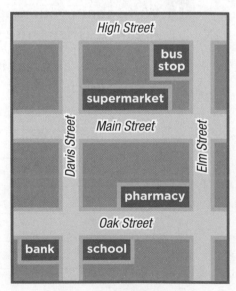

DO THE MATH Go to page 89.

A **Read the questions. Circle *yes* or *no*.**

1. Do you have an emergency exit map for your home?   yes   no

2. Are you prepared for a fire or an accident?   yes   no

B **Read the poster. What number do you call for emergencies?**

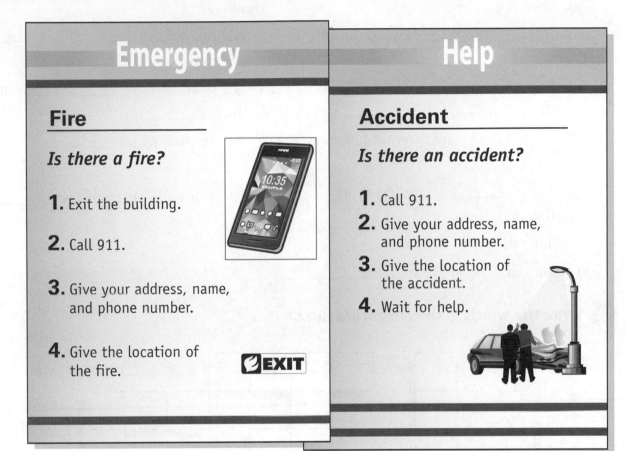

C **Look at the poster in B. Circle *a* or *b*.**

1. There's a fire. ____ the building.

   a. Give

   b. Exit

2. ____ 911.

   a. Exit

   b. Call

3. Give your address, name,

   and ____.

   a. phone number

   b. age

4. There's an accident. Call ____.

   a. help

   b. 911

5. Give the ____ of the accident.

   a. time

   b. location

6. Wait for ____.

   a. help

   b. 911

A Complete the sentences. Use the words in the box.

There	~~many~~	between	across	clinic	station
office	school	fire	bus	bank	

Across

2. How ____many____ restaurants are there?

4. There's a _____ stop on the right.

7. _____ are three ambulances on the road.

8. The _____ station is on the left.

10. Take the car to the gas _____.

11. He's sick. He's at the _____.

Down

1. The pharmacy is _____ the restaurant and the parking lot.

3. The pharmacy is _____ from the park.

5. We are studying at _____.

6. Is there a post _____ here?

9. I'm taking the check to the _____.

B Write the words in the crossword puzzle.

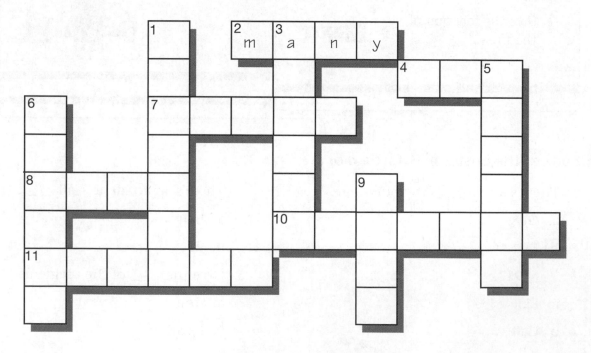

Daily Routines

A Look at the pictures. Read the activities. Check (✓) the activities you do at home. Mark (X) activities you do at work or at school. Some activities may have both a ✓ and an X.

At home

At school

do homework _____	get up _____	go to bed ___✓___	do housework _____
eat lunch _____	study _✓+X_	make dinner _____	pick up the kids _____
drink coffee _____	work _____	take a shower _____	wash dishes _____

B Choose four activities you do at home. Complete the sentences about the activities. Give the times.

I eat lunch at 12:30 p.m.

1. I _____ at _____.

2. I _____ at _____.

3. I _____ at _____.

4. I _____ at _____.

C Choose three activities you do at work or school. Complete the sentences about the activities. Give the times.

I study math at 9 a.m.

1. I _____ at _____.

2. I _____ at _____.

3. I _____ at _____.

A Read the work schedule.

Hotel Royale
Daily Work Schedule: Oscar LaPlante

2nd Shift: 4:00 p.m. to 12:00 a.m.	Work days: Thursday to Sunday
Time	**Job**
4:00 p.m. to 6:00 p.m.	wash the tables
6:00 p.m. to 8:00 p.m.	mop the floors
8:00 p.m. to 8:30 p.m.	eat dinner
8:30 p.m. to 12:00 a.m.	wash the dishes/ help the manager

B Look at the work schedule in A. Complete the sentences.

1. My name is Oscar LaPlante. I work at the _____ Hotel Royale _____ .

2. I work four days a week, from Thursday to _____.

3. I work from _____ to midnight.

4. I _____ from 4:00 to 6:00.

5. From 6:00 to 8:00, I _____.

6. I _____ at 8:00 with my friend Alfredo.

7. At 8:30, I _____ and help _____.

8. I go home at _____. My family is sleeping!

C Check (✓) the things you do at work or at home. Then choose three activities. Write sentences. Write the day and time.

At work or at home?					
	Work	Home		Work	Home
wash windows		(✓)	mop the floor		
wash the dishes			answer the phone		
use a copy machine			have lunch		

I wash windows on Saturday at noon.

1. _____

2. _____

3. _____

A **Look at the pictures. Read the days. Complete the sentences.**

Linda

Pat

Maria and Lisa

Saturday and Sunday   Tuesday and Thursday   Monday and Tuesday

1. On Saturday and Sunday, Linda _____visits_____ a friend.

2. On Monday and Tuesday, Maria _____ TV.

3. Lisa _____ on Monday and Tuesday.

4. Pat _____ the kids to the park on Tuesday and Thursday.

5. He _____ with the kids in the park.

6. Linda _____ in the park on Saturday and Sunday.

B **Read Linda's paragraph.**

I live in San Jose. I work on the weekends. I ride the bus to work in the morning. Some days, I visit a friend after work. Her name is Judy. We listen to music and talk for hours. We exercise in the park.

C **Look at the paragraph in B. Answer the information questions. Use complete sentences and the simple present.**

1. Where does Linda live?

   Linda lives in San Jose.

2. When does she work?

   _____

3. When does she ride the bus?

   _____

4. When does she visit Judy?

   _____

D Complete the questions about Jon and Monica. Use *do* or *does*. Then answer the questions.

8 a.m. to 4 p.m.

8 a.m. to 4 p.m.

4 p.m. to 6 p.m.

6 p.m. to 7 p.m.

8 p.m. to 10 p.m.

8 p.m. to 2 a.m.

1. When _____does_____ Jon work? _He works from 8 a.m. to 4 p.m._____

2. When _____ Monica do housework? _____

3. When _____ they exercise? _____

4. When _____ they eat dinner? _____

5. When _____ Jon do housework? _____

6. When _____ Monica work? _____

E Answer the questions. Use complete sentences in the simple present.

1. What time do you have lunch on Mondays?

_____

2. What time do you go to bed on Saturdays?

_____

3. What time do you get up on Sundays?

_____

A Match the pictures with the sentences.

___d___ 1. Put the paper in the printer.

_____ 2. Push this button.

_____ 3. Fill the stapler.

_____ 4. Turn on the computer.

B Complete the conversation. Use the words in the box.

problem	the paper here	help me	my job	~~Excuse me~~	fill the

A: _Excuse me_____, Ms. Jones. Can you _____?
　　　　　　　1　　　　　　　　　　　　　　　　　　　　　　　2

B: Yes? What is it?

A: How do I _____ copy machine?
　　　　　　　　　　3

B: Let me see. Put _____.
　　　　　　　　　　　　4

A: Oh. Thank you.

B: No _____. That's _____.
　　　　　　　5　　　　　　　　　　　　　　　　　　　　6

C Look at the underlined word. Write the object pronoun.

1. Please tell <u>Maria</u>.　　　　　　　→　　Please tell _her_____.

2. Could you help <u>me and my friend</u>?　→　　Could you help _____?

3. Can you show <u>Bob and Monica</u>?　→　　Can you show _____?

4. Please call <u>your parents</u>.　　　　→　　Please call _____.

5. Can you ask <u>John</u> for help?　　　→　　Can you ask _____ for help?

6. Give this to <u>Mrs. Guan</u>.　　　　→　　Give this to _____.

A Read the article. Are people busy?

Family Time

Is family important? Is there time for family?

Look at the number of hours in a day. Do parents have time to spend with their children? Many parents work for about ten hours each day. Then they do housework for about two hours and sleep for about eight hours. There are four hours left for the children.

The children are also busy. They are at school in the day. They also have homework at night. They also like computers, television, and video games. There are only about two hours left for family.

Is family important? Yes, it is! Is there time for family? That is the question!

B Look at the article in A. Circle *a* or *b*.

1. Who is busy?
   a. parents only
   (b.) parents and children

2. How many hours do parents work each day?
   a. 4
   b. 10

3. What do children have at night?
   a. homework
   b. housework

4. How many hours are left for families?
   a. 2
   b. 10

5. This article says _____.
   a. families aren't important
   b. families are important

C Answer the questions. Use your own information. Use complete sentences.

How many hours do you work? I work seven hours every day.

1. How many hours do you work?

   _____

2. How many hours do you sleep at night?

   _____

3. How many hours do you spend with your family?

   _____

A **Unscramble the words. Complete the sentences.**

1. At work, I ____answer____ the phone. (sranwe)

2. We _____ home from work at 5:30 p.m. (meco)

3. They _____ the dishes in the morning. (ashw)

4. What time do you _____ up? (egt)

5. I _____ coffee in the morning. (knird)

6. We _____ at school. (dsuty)

7. At work, they _____ the manager. (phel)

8. At 7:00 p.m., I _____ dinner. (aekm)

B **Write the words from A in the puzzle.**

8:00 AM
9:30 AM
6:00 PM
7:30 PM
6:00 AM
8:30 AM
5:00 PM
1:30 PM
7:00 AM
8:30 AM
4:00 PM
5:30 PM

1. a n s w e r
2. _ _ _ _
3. _ _ _ _
4. _ _ _
5. _ _ _ _ _
6. _ _ _ _ _
7. _ _ _ _
8. _ _ _ _

C **Look at the letters in the boxes in B. What's the secret word?**

s __ __ __ __ __ __ __
1 2 3 4 5 6 7 8

UNIT 7 Shop and Spend

LESSON 1 VOCABULARY

A Match the amounts of money with the pictures.

 ①
 ②
 ③
 ④

 ⑤
⑥
⑦
⑧

____ 25¢	____ $5.00	____ $1.00	____ 75¢
____ 1¢	_1_ 5¢	____ 10¢	____ 50¢

B Look at the pictures. Answer the questions. Use complete sentences.

The Fashion Barn

$16.00
$12.00
$75.00
$25.00
$45.00
$18.00
$34.00
$8.50
$17.50
$2.25

1. How much is the T-shirt?

   It's $8.50.

2. How much is the tie?

   _____

3. How much are the woman's shoes?

   _____

4. How much is the suit?

   _____

5. How much is the dress?

   _____

6. How much are the socks?

   _____

7. How much are the pants?

   _____

8. How much is the blouse?

   _____

A Look at Saera's chart. Mark the sentences *T* (true) or *F* (false).

Clothes Saera needs	Places Saera shops	Ways Saera pays
pants	Value Discount Store	debit card
sweater	online	cash

_F_ 1. Saera needs a dress.

____ 2. Saera shops online.

____ 3. Saera pays with a credit card.

____ 4. Saera needs pants.

____ 5. Saera pays with cash.

B Look at Saera's chart in A. Answer the questions. Use complete sentences.

1. What does Saera need? _She needs pants and a sweater._____

2. Where does Saera shop? _____

3. How does Saera pay? _____

C Complete your clothes chart. Then complete the paragraph.

Clothes I need	Places I shop	Ways I pay

I need _____ and _____. I shop
at _____ and _____. I pay with
_____ and _____.

A Match the questions with the answers.

_c_ 1. Do you want a new car?   a. No, she doesn't.

____ 2. Do we need a new car?   b. Yes, they do.

____ 3. Does Philippe have a jacket?   c. Yes, I do.

____ 4. Does Sharon need some paper?   d. Yes, you do.

____ 5. Do Mark and Adam have books?   e. Yes, he does.

____ 6. Do I need a sweater today?   f. No, we don't.

B Complete the questions. Use *do* or *does*. Then answer the questions.

1. **A:** __Does__ Sharon like to shop?

   B: Yes, ____she does____.

2. **A:** _____ Sharon want to buy the skirt?

   B: No, _____.

3. **A:** _____ Roberto have cash?

   B: No, _____.

4. **A:** _____ Roberto need a jacket?

   B: Yes, _____.

5. **A:** _____ the salespeople help the customers?

   B: Yes, _____.

6. **A:** _____ you like to shop?

   B: Yes, _____.

C Look at the pictures. Complete the sentences. Use *need, want,* or *have.*

1. Hetal and his wife _____have_____ a small apartment.

2. They _____ to buy a new house.

3. They _____ a lot of money for the house.

4. Nancy _____ a bicycle.

5. She _____ a new car.

6. Nancy _____ $20,000 for the car.

D Write simple present *yes/no* questions. Use the words in parentheses.

1. **A:** _Do the children need new jackets?_____ (the children / need / new jackets)

   B: No, they need new shoes.

2. **A:** _____ (John / want / a new house)

   B: No, he has a nice apartment.

3. **A:** _____ (Sara / want / the blue blouse)

   B: No, she wants the red blouse.

4. **A:** _____ (you / want / the green sweater)

   B: No, I don't like it.

E Complete the questions and answers. Use *do, does, have,* or *has.*

1. **A:** _Does_____ Ana have some cash?

   B: No, but she ____has____ a debit card.

2. **A:** _____ Sara and Philippe have a debit card?

   B: No, but they _____ a credit card.

3. **A:** _____ your friends have a new house?

   B: No, but they _____ a new car.

4. **A:** _____ your neighbor have a new car?

   B: No, he doesn't _____ a new car.

A Match the parts of the conversation.

_b_ 1. Would you like to try on that sweatshirt?

____ 2. What size do you need?

____ 3. How much is this jacket?

____ 4. Here's a large in blue.

____ 5. How much are these gloves?

a. Okay. Thank you! I'll take it!

b. Yes, please.

c. They're on sale for $12.

d. I need a small.

e. It's on sale for $39.

B Complete the conversation. Use the words in the box.

| Here's   take it   ~~Excuse~~   How much   What size   on sale |

A: _Excuse_____ me. _____ is this shirt?

B: It's _____ for $14.95. _____ do you need?

A: I need a small.

B: _____ a small in blue.

A: Okay. I'll _____.

C Look at the order form. Answer the questions. Use complete sentences.

Item	Item Number	Size	Color	Price	Number	Total
sweater	210543	M	White	16.95	2	$33.90
gloves	712288	M	Green	12.95	1	$12.95
jacket	342995	L	Blue	24.95	1	$24.95

1. What color are the sweaters? _They're white._____

2. How much is one sweater? _____

3. How many sweaters does the customer want? _____

4. How much are the gloves? _____

5. What size is the jacket? _____

DO THE MATH Go to page 90.

A **Match the words and the definitions.**

_____ 1. fees

_____ 2. purchases

_____ 3. due date

a. things that you buy

b. the last day you can pay your bill

c. extra money the credit card company adds to your bill

B **Read the article. Are credit cards always bad?**

Tips for Using Credit Cards

Do you have a credit card? Do you sometimes pay fees to the credit card company? Read these tips for using credit cards.

✓ Always pay the total amount of your bill.

✓ Pay your bill on time. Never pay late.

✓ Check your account online. You can see how much you are spending.

✓ Only use your credit card for big purchases. Use cash for small purchases.

✓ Pay your bill at a good time of the month for you. For example, after you get paid.

Remember, credit cards can be your friend. Just follow these tips!

C **Look at the article in B. Circle the correct words.**

1. Pay the ((total) / partial) amount of your bill.

2. Pay your bill (late / on time).

3. Check your account (in person / online).

4. Use cash for (big / small) purchases.

5. Pay your bill at a (good / bad) time of month for you.

A Circle the letter of the correct answer.

A Secret Message

1. How much is the blouse?
   I. $15   B. Small

2. What color do you want?
   A. Yes, I do.   T. Blue

3. Does Tomas need a jacket?
   R. Yes, they do.   S. No, he doesn't.

4. What size do you need?
   O. Medium   P. It's perfect.

5. Are there any shoes on sale?
   N. Yes, there are.   O. Yes, there is.

6. What do you wear at home?
   U. Yes, I do.   S. Pants and a T-shirt

7. Is there an ATM in the store?
   A. Yes, there is.   B. No, it isn't.

8. Do Mike and Sara have a new car?
   K. Yes, he does.   L. No, they don't.

9. How much are the socks?
   I. It's $4.   E. They're $3.50.

B Write the letters from the answers in A. Read the message.

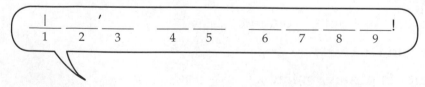

$$\frac{|}{1} \, \underline{}_{2} \, {}^{'} \underline{}_{3} \quad \underline{}_{4} \, \underline{}_{5} \quad \underline{}_{6} \, \underline{}_{7} \, \underline{}_{8} \, \underline{}_{9}!$$

A **Complete the sentences. Use the words in the box.**

| ~~cart~~ basket cashier bagger aisle |

1. Joe is buying a lot of food. He's using a _____*cart*_____.

2. Rita is only buying two or three things. She has a small _____.

3. The _____ is putting the potatoes into a bag.

4. The bread is in _____ 1, next to the cookies.

5. The _____ is working at the cash register.

B **Match the words with the pictures.**

①    ②    ③

④    ⑤    ⑥

⑦    ⑧    ⑨

___ bananas   ___ milk   ___ potatoes   ___ apples   ___ lettuce

___ tomatoes   ___ eggs   _1_ grapes   ___ onions

C **Circle *a* or *b*.**

1. A ____ works in a supermarket.
   a. bagger   b. customer

2. People use ____ in the store.
   a. baskets   b. cars

3. Onions and ____ are vegetables.
   a. bread   b. lettuce

4. Grapes and bananas are ____.
   a. vegetables   b. fruit

A Complete the sentences. Use the words in the box.

a customer	~~a cashier~~	good prices
a shopping list	once a week	is buying

1. My name is Sasha. I work here at Save More Supermarket.

   I'm _____a cashier_____.

2. Here comes Mr. Singh. He's _____ here.

3. He brings _____ with him every time he shops.

4. Today, he _____ fruit, vegetables, and fish.

5. Mr. Singh buys fish _____. We have fresh fish every Thursday.

6. Mr. Singh is a good shopper. He always looks for _____.

B Look at the pictures. Write the shopping list for each person. Use the words in the box.

bananas	bread	potatoes	chicken	cookies	fish
eggs	~~lettuce~~	milk	ice cream	rice	grapes

lettuce

A Read the calendar.

October 2006

Sunday	Monday	Tuesday	Wednesday	Thursday	Friday	Saturday
1 exercise, study	**2** work, exercise	**3** work, exercise, visit Louis	**4** work, exercise, cook dinner	**5** shopping, exercise, cook dinner	**6** visit parents, exercise	**7** clean apt., shopping, exercise
8	**9**	**10**	**11**	**12**	**13**	**14**

B Look at the calendar in A. Complete the sentences. Use the words in the box.

three times   twice a week   never   every day

1. Helen works _____three times_____ a week.

2. She exercises _____.

3. Helen goes shopping _____.

4. Helen _____ eats out on Wednesdays.

C Unscramble the sentences.

1. dinner / cook / We / at / always / home
   We always cook dinner at home._____

2. ice cream / eat / I / never

   _____

3. Paula / a / once / pizza / eats / week

   _____

4. month / friends / times / They / a / have / with / dinner / four

   _____

D Complete the sentences. Use your own information.

I cook dinner six times a week.

1. I cook dinner _____.

2. I order pizza _____.

3. I eat dinner with friends _____.

E Look at the chart. Read the questions. Check (✓) the correct answers. Use your own information.

How Often Do You Do These Things?

	every day	once a week	once a month	once or twice a year	never
1. How often do you go shopping?					
2. How often do you eat fish?					
3. How often do you eat lunch with your family?					
4. How often do you go to a restaurant for breakfast?					

F Look at the chart in E. Write sentences.

I go shopping once a week.

1. _____

2. _____

3. _____

4. _____

G Read the Grammar note. Then write sentences with *always, usually, sometimes,* or *never*. Use your own information.

Grammar note			
always	usually	sometimes	never
100%	70%	30%	0%

I usually study English in the evening.

1. study English / the evening

_____

2. ride / the bus

_____

3. get up / 7 a.m.

_____

4. go to bed / 8 p.m.

_____

LESSON **4** EVERYDAY CONVERSATION

A **Complete the conversation. Use the words in the box.**

~~ready to order~~	I'd like	that's one	anything to drink
I do	coffee too	right	please

Server: Are you _____ready to order_____?

1

Beena: Yes, we are. _____ a

2

chicken sandwich, _____.

3

Server: Do you want _____?

4

Beena: Yes, _____. I'd like some

5

coffee.

Server: And you?

Carl: Some vegetable soup and a salad. No onions

in the salad, please.

Server: Anything to drink?

Carl: I'd like _____, please.

6

Server: Okay, _____ chicken sandwich, vegetable soup,

7

and a salad with no onions, and two cups of coffee.

Beena: That's _____.

8

B **Match the food order with the confirmation.**

_c_ 1. I'd like the chicken with rice
and vegetables.

____ 2. I need a bag of apples.

____ 3. I need five potatoes.

____ 4. Can I have a small coffee?

____ 5. I'd like a pizza with pepperoni,
mushrooms, and onions, please.

a. I'm sorry. What size?

b. I'm sorry. How many potatoes?

c. That's the chicken with rice and
vegetables, right?

d. That's pepperoni, mushrooms,
and onions, right?

e. Red or green apples?

A Read the article. What food is it about?

Is Pizza Healthy?

Many people say, "Pizza is not a healthy food." Other people say, "Pizza is good for you." Think about it. Pizza can be good for you.

- Order pizza with vegetables on it. You can order pizza with tomatoes, peppers, onions, and mushrooms.

- Don't order pizza with pepperoni. Order pizza with chicken. Pepperoni has a lot salt, but chicken doesn't. A lot of salt is unhealthy.

- Some places have pizza with pineapple on it. Pineapple is a fruit. Order pineapple pizza to be healthy.

So you see, pizza can be a healthy food!

Pineapples

B Look at the article in A. Circle *a* or *b*.

1. Pizza with vegetables on it is _____.
   a. healthy
   b. unhealthy

2. Sue wants pizza with vegetables.
   She can order _____.
   a. pizza with peppers and mushrooms
   b. pizza with chicken and pineapple

3. Paul wants pizza with only a
   little salt. He can order _____.
   a. pizza with pepperoni
   b. pizza with chicken

4. Pineapple pizza is _____.
   a. healthy
   b. unhealthy

5. Pizza is _____ healthy.
   a. always
   b. sometimes

Find the Differences

Look at the pictures. Alicia and Frank do different things for lunch on Thursdays and Fridays. Find the differences. Complete the sentences.

1. On Thursdays, Alicia and Frank eat lunch at ___12 p.m.___

   On Fridays, they eat lunch at ___1 p.m.___

2. On Thursdays, Alicia drinks _____.

   On Fridays, she drinks _____.

3. On Thursdays, Frank eats _____.

   On Fridays, he eats _____ and a _____.

4. On Thursdays, Alicia eats _____, french fries, and a _____.

   On Fridays, she eats _____ and a potato.

5. On Thursdays, Frank drinks a _____ soda.

   On Fridays, he drinks a _____ soda.

UNIT 9 Your Health

LESSON 1 VOCABULARY

A Look at the picture. Match the words with the picture. Use the words in the box.

~~mouth~~	leg	head	arm	neck	nose	foot	hand	chest	knee

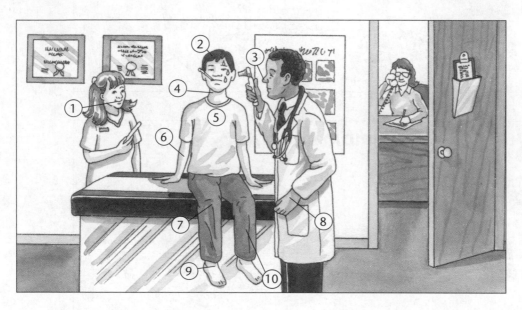

1. ___mouth___   4. _____   7. _____   10. _____

2. _____   5. _____   8. _____

3. _____   6. _____   9. _____

B Look at the picture in A. Complete the sentences. Use the words in the box.

doctor	fever	receptionist	earache	~~patient~~	nurse

1. What's the matter with the _____patient_____?

2. He has an _____.

3. He has a _____ too.

4. The _____ is looking at his ear.

5. The _____ is answering the telephone.

6. The _____ is helping the doctor.

58   Unit 9 Lesson 1

A **Complete the story. Use the words in the box.**

examines her	drinks some	to the doctor	her temperature	a prescription
~~sick~~	sore throat	goes home	the medicine	

Kim is _____sick_____ today. She has a fever and a

_____. She goes _____.
          2   3

First, the nurse takes _____. After that,
                        4

the doctor _____. The doctor writes
            5

_____. Kim _____.
      6   7

At home, she takes _____ and
                     8

_____ hot tea.
      9

B **How do you get better? Check (✓) the things you do. Then write sentences.**

For a cold, I rest and drink fluids.

What do you do for a...	rest	drink fluids	take medicine	stay home
1. cold?	✓	✓		
2. backache?				
3. headache?				
4. stomachache?				
5. earache?				
6. fever?				

1. _____

2. _____

3. _____

4. _____

5. _____

6. _____

A Complete the sentences. Use *has* or *have*.

1. I _____have_____ a headache.

2. Kim _____ a sore throat.

3. We _____ to exercise every day.

4. The doctor and nurse _____ a lot of work today.

5. You _____ to quit smoking.

6. He _____ to stay home and rest.

B Complete the sentences. Use *have/has* or *have to/has to*.

1. I _____have_____ a headache. I ___have to___ rest.

2. Lily _____ go to the dentist. She _____ a toothache.

3. Paul _____ a broken leg. He _____ stay home.

4. They _____ drink fluids and rest. They _____ colds.

5. You _____ a fever. You _____ go to the doctor.

C Unscramble the questions. Then complete the answers. Use *have/has* or *have to/has to*.

1. you / have / study / to / do / Why

   A: _Why do you have to study?_____

   B: I _____have_____ a test tomorrow.

2. does / take / Why / he / have / to / medicine

   A: _____

   B: He _____ a cold.

3. they / store / Why / do / to / go / to / have / the

   A: _____

   B: They _____ buy some food.

4. every / day / Why / she / does / have / to / run

   A: _____

   B: She _____ exercise.

5. do / Why / leave / have / you / early / to

   A: _____

   B: I _____ pick up my son.

D **Complete the questions.**

1. **A:** Where _does John have to go?_____

   B: John has to go to the pharmacy.

2. **A:** What _____

   B: He has to buy some medicine.

3. **A:** Where _____

   B: They have to go to school tomorrow.

4. **A:** When _____

   B: You have to go to bed at 11 p.m.

5. **A:** How often _____

   B: She has to take the pills twice a day.

E **Look at the chart. Then rewrite the sentences with _have/has got to_.**

> **Have got to**
>
> In conversation, people often use _have got to_ or _has got to_ instead of _have to_ or _has to_. The meaning is the same.
>
> I **have got to** work. = I **have to** work.
>
> She **has got to** study. = She **has to** study.

1. We have to go to the dentist soon.

   _We have got to go to the dentist soon._____

2. You have to take your medicine.

   _____

3. The teacher has to leave early tonight.

   _____

4. They have to work this weekend.

   _____

5. I have to stay home. I have a fever.

   _____

6. You have to exercise more.

   _____

A Read the appointment card. Answer the questions.

1. Who has an appointment?

   Rick DeSoto

2. What day is the appointment?

   _____

3. What time is the appointment?

   _____

4. What's the date of the appointment?

   _____

Dentist Appointment
Patient: ___Rick DeSoto___
Has an appointment on: _Monday, May 23_
At: _11:00_ (a.m.) p.m.
With: ___Dr. Silver___
Please call (978) 555-3730 to cancel your appointment.

B Complete the conversation. Use the words in the box.

it is	9 a.m.	Tuesday, October 5th
~~see the dentist~~	that OK	has an opening

A: Can I help you?

B: My name is Karen Hill. I have to _____see the dentist_____ in six months.
                                                         1

A: Let's see. Dr. Durgin _____ on October 5th at 9 a.m.
                                                    2

   Is _____?
        3

B: Yes, _____. Thanks.
             4

A: OK. See you on _____ at _____.
                              5   6

C Look at the conversation in B. Complete the appointment card.

Dentist Appointment

Patient: _____

Has an appointment on: _____

At: _____ a.m. p.m.

With: _____

Please call (978) 555-3730 to cancel your appointment.

DO THE MATH Go to page 91.

A Read the article. What makes chicken soup healthy?

Health Note of the Day
Chicken Soup: It's Good Medicine!

My grandmother says chicken soup is good for people with colds. Now doctors are finding that chicken soup is good medicine. The hot steam helps you. There are onions, carrots, and other vegetables in chicken soup that help you. Bananas, oranges, and tea are good for colds too.

Do you have a cold? Listen to your grandmother! Have some chicken soup.

B Look at the article in A. Mark the sentences *T* (true) or *F* (false).

_T_ 1. The writer's grandmother says chicken soup is good for colds.

____ 2. Now doctors think that chicken soup is bad for colds.

____ 3. The steam of the soup can help.

____ 4. The fruit in chicken soup helps you.

____ 5. You have a cold. You should go to the pharmacy.

C Read the medicine label. Answer the questions.

1. How many pills does she take every day?

   _____ two _____

2. How often does she take this medicine?

   _____

3. Should she take this medicine with food?

   _____

4. How many refills are there?

   _____

 NEWVILLE PHARMACY

4411468   DR.EDWARDS
NOVAK,PAULINA 07-05-18
TAKE ONE PILL TWICE A DAY.
*WARNING: Take with food.
ONE REFILL

A Go around the spiral. Find eight things a doctor says. Write them on the lines below. Use complete sentences.

1. <u>Go home and drink juice.</u>
2. _____
3. _____
4. _____
5. _____
6. _____
7. _____
8. _____

B Create your own "sentence spiral." Bring it to class. Then ask your classmates to find the sentences.

10 Getting the Job

LESSON 1 VOCABULARY

A Who says these things? Write the jobs. Use the words in the box.

childcare worker	~~server~~	physician assistant	plumber	delivery person	cook

1. I serve food in a restaurant. — _server_

2. I help the doctors at a hospital. — _____

3. I take care of children. — _____

4. I make food for my job. — _____

5. I deliver packages. — _____

6. I fix sinks. — _____

B What do they do? Where do they work? Complete the sentences with the job and the place.

1. Yolanda's a _____gardener_____.

   She works in a _____.

2. Mark's an _____.

   He works in a _____.

A **Read the job ads. Answer the questions.**

1. What's the job in ad A?

_____server_____

2. Is this job full-time or part-time?

_____

3. Is the job in the mornings or in the evenings?

_____

4. What's the job in ad B?

_____

5. Where is the job?

_____

6. Is this a full-time or part-time job?

_____

A

> **———— Servers Needed————**
>
> Lisa's Restaurant is looking for servers.
> Evenings, PT (18 hours a week).
> Call Fred: 555-1302

B

> **‾Work at Children's Castle!‾**
>
> Childcare Worker at Children's Castle
> FT (40 hours a week). Call Danielle for
> an application: 555-2212

B **Read the story. Complete the sentences. Use the words in the box.**

as a bus driver	in person	online	interview for the job
full-time	~~job~~	job listings	completes a form

Ben was a truck driver in Mexico. Now he lives in

Chicago. He's looking for a _____job_____.
                                     1

First, he looks _____,
                              2

but he doesn't find a job. Then he looks at the

_____ in the newspaper.
              3

There is an ad for a _____ job
                                   4

_____. He calls about the job. He
              5

has to apply for the job _____.
                                        6

He goes to the office of the bus company and

_____. Later, he has an
              7

_____. Now Ben has a new job!
              8

A Look at the timeline. Complete the sentences. Use *was* or *were*.

1997	2011	2014	2017

POLAND   **NEW JERSEY**

Stan- *student*   Stan- *cook*   Stan- *cook*
Marie- *student*   Marie- *dental assistant*   Marie- *childcare worker*

In 1997, Stan and I _____were_____ in Poland.
                              1
Stan _____ a student for 14 years. I
                2
_____ also a student. From 2011 to 2013, we _____
        3   4
not students. I _____ a dental assistant, and Stan
                        5
_____ a cook. In 2014, we _____ not in Poland.
        6   7
We _____ in New Jersey.
        8

B Look at the timeline in A. Complete the questions. Use *was* or *were*.
Write short answers.

1. **A:** _Was_____ Stan a student in 2013?

   B: _No, he wasn't._____

2. **A:** _____ Stan and Marie in Poland in 2000?

   B: _____

3. **A:** _____ they in school from 2011 to 2017?

   B: _____

4. **A:** _____ Marie a dental assistant from 2013 to 2017?

   B: _____

5. **A:** In 2013, _____ Stan a cook?

   B: _____

6. **A:** _____ they in New Jersey in 2016?

   B: _____

C Write sentences. Use the simple past with *be*.

1. Min and Hung-ju / students / in Korea

   <u>Min and Hung-ju were students in Korea.</u>

2. They / students / from 2005 to 2011

   _____

3. Min / a home health aide / from 2011 to 2013

   _____

4. Hung-ju / not / a teacher / in Korea

   _____

5. Min and Hung-ju / in San Francisco / last year

   _____

6. Min / not / in Korea / last year

   _____

D Read about Ana. Then complete the questions and short answers. Use *is*, *was*, or *does*. Use complete sentences.

> Ana was a student in El Salvador for 14 years, from 1997 to 2011. After that, she was a teacher for four years in the capital city, San Salvador. She was there from 2012 to 2016. Then she was in Florida for one year. Now, she's in Arlington, Virginia. She has a job. She's a childcare worker.

1. A: <u>Was</u> Ana a student in El Salvador?

   B: <u>Yes, she was.</u> _____

2. A: _____ she a teacher in San Salvador for four years?

   B: _____

3. A: _____ she in Florida for two years?

   B: _____

4. A: _____ she in Florida now?

   B: _____

5. A: _____ she have a job now?

   B: _____

A **Complete the conversation. Use the words in the box.**

You're hired	can use	I do	an office manager
I can	work experience	~~Tell me~~	weekends

A: <u>Tell me</u> about yourself, Ms. Singh.
        1

B: I'm from India. I came here six years ago.

A: Do you have any _____?
                            2

B: Yes, _____. I was _____ from 2003
                 3   4

    to 2008 in India. In 2012, I was an office worker in Charleston.

    I _____ a computer and photocopier. I like to work with people.
               5

A: Can you work _____?
                      6

B: Yes, _____.
          7

A: That's great. _____.
                  8

B **Look at the conversation in A. Complete the application form.**

JOB APPLICATION

Position: Office Manager

Applicant Name: Anita Singh

Experience:

Job Title	Number of Years	Location
		India
		Charleston

Skills: Please check (✓) the skills you have

☐ use a computer   ☐ drive   ☐ fix office machines

☐ make copies   ☐ answer phones   ☐ other

Submit

A Read the article and the timecard app. Why does the Top Star Hotel use a timecard app?

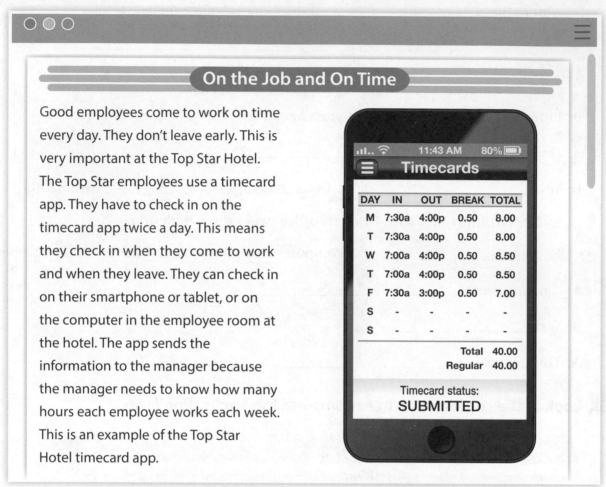

On the Job and On Time

Good employees come to work on time every day. They don't leave early. This is very important at the Top Star Hotel. The Top Star employees use a timecard app. They have to check in on the timecard app twice a day. This means they check in when they come to work and when they leave. They can check in on their smartphone or tablet, or on the computer in the employee room at the hotel. The app sends the information to the manager because the manager needs to know how many hours each employee works each week. This is an example of the Top Star Hotel timecard app.

DAY	IN	OUT	BREAK	TOTAL
M	7:30a	4:00p	0.50	8.00
T	7:30a	4:00p	0.50	8.00
W	7:00a	4:00p	0.50	8.50
T	7:00a	4:00p	0.50	8.50
F	7:30a	3:00p	0.50	7.00
S	-	-	-	-
S	-	-	-	-
			Total	40.00
			Regular	40.00

Timecard status:
SUBMITTED

B Look at the article in A. Mark the sentences *T* (true) or *F* (false).

___T___ 1. Good employees are on time for work every day.

_____ 2. Good employees often leave early.

_____ 3. The Top Star Hotel employees use a timecard app.

_____ 4. Employees can only check in on smartphones.

_____ 5. In the example, the employee usually finishes work at 4:00 p.m.

_____ 6. On Wednesday, the employee was at work at 2:00 p.m.

_____ 7. From Monday to Friday, the employee was at work for 40 hours.

_____ 8. On Friday, the employee was at work at 8:00 p.m.

A **Unscramble the words.**

Jobs and Work Places

1. u o t a   c h a m e i c n   auto mechanic
2. e r g a g a   _____
3. r e v e r s   _____
4. t e s t a r n u a r   _____
5. d e n s r a g   _____
6. d a r n e r e g   _____
7. t l h p i s o a   _____
8. n h y p s i i a c   t n s a s i a s t   _____

B **Complete the chart. Use the words in the box.**

physician assistant	office	kitchen	manager	gardener	garage
~~auto mechanic~~	garden	restaurant	hospital	cook	server

Jobs	Workplaces	Skills
auto mechanic		fixes cars
		helps doctors
		plants flowers
		serves food
		cooks food
		manages a business

C **Write sentences. Use the information in the chart.**

1. An auto mechanic works in a garage and fixes cars.
2. _____
3. _____
4. _____
5. _____
6. _____

A Look at the pictures. Write the words. Use the words in the box.

turn   road work   school crossing   ~~no parking~~   no left turn   speed limit

1. _____no parking_____

2. _____

3. _____

4. _____

5. _____

6. _____

B Cross out (X) the item that does NOT belong in each group.

1. safety boots   hard hat   fire extinguisher   ~~wet floor~~

2. careless   safety glasses   unsafe   dangerous

3. white   orange   safe   black

4. safety boots   factory worker   safety gloves   hard hat

C Complete the sentences. Use the words in the box.

dangerous   careless   emergency exit   ~~careful~~

1. Matt is _____careful_____. He wears a hard hat.

2. Savan doesn't wear a hard hat. She is _____.

3. That building is not safe. It's _____!

4. We have to leave the building. Where's the _____?

A Look at the picture. Check (✓) the rules people are following. Mark (X) the rules people are not following.

____ 1. Be careful with chemicals.

____ 2. Wear safety boots.

____ 3. Don't walk on a wet floor.

____ 4. Wear a hard hat.

____ 5. Wear safety glasses.

____ 6. Wear safety gloves.

B Read the chart about Nate's driving. Then complete the sentences using the information in the chart.

	always	usually	sometimes	never
1. wear a seat belt	✓			
2. obey the speed limit		✓		
3. stop at school crossings	✓			
4. park in a no-parking area				✓
5. text while driving			✓	

Nate is usually a careful driver. He _____always wears_____ a seat belt.
                                                                1

He _____ the speed limit. He _____ at
            2   3

school crossings. He _____ in a no-parking area. But he does
                                    4

one very dangerous thing. He _____ while driving.
                                              5

A Look at the picture. Complete the sentences. Use *should* or *shouldn't*.

1. Li ___should___ stay home.

2. She _____ drink tea.

3. She _____ go to work today.

4. She _____ take some medicine.

5. She _____ visit her friends.

6. She _____ rest in bed.

B Linda's neighborhood isn't safe. Write sentences about Linda. Use the words in parentheses and *should* or *shouldn't*. What should Linda do? What shouldn't she do?

1. (lock the door)

   She should lock the door.

2. (walk alone at night)

   _____

3. (say hello to her neighbors)

   _____

4. (open the door to strangers)

   _____

5. (leave the building door open)

   _____

C Complete the questions.

1. A: What _should I do?_

   B: You should go home.

2. A: What _____

   B: He should turn right.

3. A: How often _____

   B: They should always wear a seat belt.

4. A: How often _____

   B: You should obey the laws every day.

D Complete the sentences. Use *should* or *shouldn't* and the verbs in the box.

drive	stop	talk	wear	~~slow down~~

1. The driver __should slow down__ near the school.

2. He _____ at the traffic light.

3. He _____ his seat belt.

4. He _____ on his cell phone.

5. He _____ 80 mph.

E Complete the conversation. Use *should* or *shouldn't* and the verbs in parentheses.

Olivia: Hi, I'm Olivia. I'm a new student in this class. Our teacher, Mr. Lewis, wants me to learn the classroom rules. Can you help me?

Dan: Hi, Olivia. It's nice to meet you. Well, one important rule in this class is to be on time. You __shouldn't be late__ (be late) to class.
1

Sara: Hi, Olivia. I'm Sara. You _____ (speak) English at home,
2
and you _____ (sleep) in class.
3

Dan: Oh, and you _____ (do) your homework, and you
4
_____ (forget) your books.
5

Sara: And one more rule. You _____ (have fun)!
6

Olivia: OK, thanks for your help!

F Complete the sentences. Use *should* or *have to.*

1. You can't park in front of the school. You
   _____have to_____ park in the parking lot.

2. I think you _____ listen to the radio.
   It helps you learn English.

3. Where is your hard hat? You _____
   wear a hard hat in this work area. It's the rule.

4. Don't forget! You _____ pay the
   electric bill today. It's very important!

5. I think you _____ get more exercise.
   It's good for you.

> **Need help?**
>
> **should vs. have to**
> should = It's a good idea.
> have to = It's necessary.

A Complete the conversation. Use the words in the box.

a car accident	anyone hurt	the address
~~Emergency~~	ambulance	should I do

A: 911. _____Emergency_____.
   ₁

B: Help! There is _____ across the street from my house!
   ₂

A: OK. What's _____?
   ₃

B: It's 932 Eastside Drive.

A: Is _____?
   ₄

B: I don't know. I can't see them. I think so. The people can't get out of the car.

A: OK. Help is on the way.

B: What _____?
   ₅

A: Nothing. Stay there. Wait for the _____ and fire trucks.
   ₆

B Match the questions with the answers.

_d_ 1. Who needs help?   a. It's at 54 Highland Avenue.

____ 2. What's the emergency?   b. Yes, you should.

____ 3. Where's the emergency?   c. Someone's breaking their window.

____ 4. Should I call 911?   d. My neighbors.

C Look at the picture. You're talking to a 911 operator. Answer the questions.

1. What's the emergency?

   There's a car accident.

2. Where's the emergency?

   _____

3. Who needs help?

   _____

4. Should Sonya wait for help?

   _____

A Read the article. Are bicycles always dangerous for children?

SAFETY  FIRST

Every month at *Parents and Kids* magazine, we give you safety information. We want your children to be safe.
This month, we are giving you information on bicycle safety. Here are some ways to protect your children:

- Your children should wear bicycle helmets.

- They should not ride their bicycles at night.

- In the daytime, they should wear clothing with colors like red and yellow. This helps other people see them.

- Do you ride a bicycle? You should wear a helmet and colorful clothing. Your children see you as an example.

Every month we ask you some safety questions on the Internet. Here are our questions and your answers:

Do your children wear bicycle helmets?

64% Yes   36% No

Do you wear a bicycle helmet?

12% Yes   88% No

helmet

B Look at the article in A. Mark the sentences *T* (true) or *F* (false).

__T__ 1. This month, the magazine is about bicycle safety.

____ 2. Bicycle helmets don't protect children.

____ 3. In the daytime, children should wear colors like red or yellow.

____ 4. Parents should wear bicycle helmets too.

____ 5. Thirty-five percent of children wear bicycle helmets.

____ 6. Parents always wear helmets.

A Complete the puzzle.

Missing Letters and Secret Message

1. <u>s</u> <u>a</u> <u>f</u> <u>e</u> <u>t</u> <u>y</u> <u>b</u> <u>o</u> <u>o</u> <u>t</u> <u>s</u>

2. __ __ __ __

3. __ __ __ __ __ __ __ __ __ __ __

4. __ __ __ __ __ __

5. __ __ __ __ __ __ __

6. __ __ __ __ __ __

7. __ __ __ __ __ __ __ __ __

8. __ __ __ __ __ __ __

9. __ __ __ __ __ __

B Look at the letters in the boxes. What's the secret message?

<u>B</u> __ __ __ __ __ __ __ __ !
1 2 3 4 5 6 7 8 9

A Look at the weather map. Complete the sentences. Use the words in the box.

cloudy	~~cold~~	hot	raining	snowing	sunny

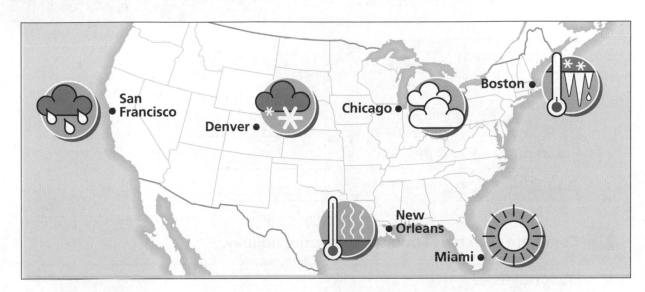

1. In Boston, it's _____cold_____.

2. In Miami, it's _____.

3. Today, it's _____ in New Orleans.

4. In Chicago, it's _____.

5. It's _____ in Denver.

6. It's _____ in San Francisco.

B Cross out (X) the words that do NOT belong.

1. fall   ~~cloudy~~   summer   winter

2. go to the beach   spring   have a picnic   go out to eat

3. summer   fall   spring   sunny

4. Father's Day   Independence Day   September   Thanksgiving

5. go to the movies go swimming   stay home   cloudy

A Read about Elisa's favorite holiday. Then complete the chart.

My favorite holiday is Mother's Day. The weather is usually warm and sunny. I spend the holiday with my mother and my sisters. This year, we're going to eat at a restaurant. Then we are going to go for a walk. I can't wait for Mother's Day!

Favorite holiday	1. _Mother's Day_
Weather	2. _____
People I'm with	3. _____
Something we're going to do – 1	4. _____
Something we're going to do – 2	5. _____

B Complete the chart about your favorite holiday.

Favorite holiday	
Weather	
People I'm with	
Something we're going to do – 1	
Something we're going to do – 2	

C Complete the paragraph about your favorite holiday. Use the information from the chart in B.

My favorite holiday is _____. The weather is usually _____. I spend the

holiday with _____. This year, we're going to _____. Then we're going to

_____. I can't wait for _____!

A **Unscramble the sentences.**

1. play / Ken / going to / baseball / is

   <u>Ken is going to play baseball.</u>

2. picnic / going to / have / We / a / are

   _____

3. am / going to / stay / I / home

   _____

4. movie / a / watch / Rita and Paul / are / going to

   _____

5. are / to / beach / You / going to / go / the

   _____

6. Isabel / going to / study / is

   _____

B **Complete the questions. Use *What*, *Who*, *When*, or *Where*. Then match the questions with the answers.**

<u> c </u> 1. <u> What   </u> are Karen and Marie going to do tonight?

_____ 2. _____ is Hector going to study?

_____ 3. _____ are Mr. and Mrs. Smith going to eat dinner with?

_____ 4. _____ is Yoshi going to go after class?

a. He's going to study on Wednesday.

b. They're going to eat dinner with their children.

c. They're going to go to the movies.

d. He's going to go to the gym.

C Write the questions. Use the future with *be going to* and *What* or *When*.

1. A: <u>When are you going to go to the beach?</u>

   B: I'm going to go to the beach <u>on Saturday</u>.

2. A: _____

   B: I'm going to <u>go swimming</u>.

3. A: _____

   B: Lucas is going to <u>visit some friends</u>.

4. A: _____

   B: We're going to study in the park <u>tomorrow</u>.

5. A: _____

   B: Eva is going to start school <u>next year</u>.

D Complete the sentences. Use the future with *be going to*.

1. I <u>work</u> on the weekend. <u>I'm going to work</u> _____ this Sunday.

2. We usually <u>play</u> tennis in the park, but tomorrow
   _____ at school.

3. Maria often <u>exercises</u> with me in the evening. Tomorrow
   _____ with me in the afternoon.

4. My friends usually <u>watch</u> a baseball game on Saturday, but
   _____ a football game this Saturday.

5. You always <u>study</u> on the weekend. _____ this
   weekend too.

E What about you? Complete the sentences. Use your own ideas.

Tonight, I'm going to clean the house and watch a movie.

1. Tonight, I'm going to _____

2. Tomorrow, _____

3. On Saturday, _____

4. Next year, _____

A Put the conversation in order. Number the sentences from 1 to 6.

_____ **B:** I'm going to go on vacation to New York.

_____ **B:** Good for you!

_____ **A:** That's great! When are you going?

_____ **A:** I'm going to take a class.

__1__ **A:** What are your plans for next summer?

_____ **B:** In July. How about you? What are your plans?

B Match the questions with the answers.

__b__ 1. Were they at work?   a. I'm going to start school.

_____ 2. What are we going to do today?   b. No, they weren't.

_____ 3. What are your plans for next year? c. We're going to go to the grocery store.

_____ 4. Was that your job before?   d. Next month.

_____ 5. When are you going to start?   e. Yes, it was.

C Unscramble the sentences in the conversation.

1. **A:** (for the summer / your plans / are / What)

   <u>What are your plans for the summer?</u>

2. **B:** (take / I'm / a class / to / going)

   _____

3. **A:** (going / are / to / What / you / class / take)

   _____

4. **B:** (a computer skills class / to / I'm / going / take)

   _____

5. **A:** (you / for / Good)

   _____

A Complete the sentences. Circle *a* or *b*.

1. A career goal is a hope you have for _____.
   a. jobs
   b. family

2. A personal goal is a hope you have for _____.
   a. jobs
   b. yourself

B Read the goal page. What are Tatiana's goals?

My Goals

Name: Tatiana Petrov

Goal:

Career

I want to be a computer technician.

Personal

I want to visit my family in Russia.

Steps:

1. I'm going to apply for school.
2. I'm going to take classes and graduate.
3. I'm going to apply for jobs.

1. I'm going to save money.
2. I'm going to make plans with my family.
3. I'm going to buy plane tickets.

C Look at the goal worksheet in B. Circle the correct words.

1. Tatiana's ((career) / personal) goal is to be a computer technician.

2. There are (three / six) steps to her career goal.

3. The third step for Tatiana's career goal is to apply for (school / jobs).

4. The first step for Tatiana's personal goal is to (visit her family / save money).

5. Tatiana is going to (buy plane tickets / take classes) as a step to meet her personal goal.

D Complete the sentences.

1. My career goal is _____.

2. My personal goal is _____.

A Find the words in the puzzle. Use the words in the box.

snowing	~~Independence Day~~	winter	New Year's Day
raining	Valentine's Day	birthday	Thanksgiving
sunny	summer	spring	fall
hot	cold	holiday	cloudy

```
W B K A N T E R F A L L O R A
I I O N E W Y E A R S D A Y V
N R T H A N K S G I V I N G A
T T Y S N W T I O P L L I C L
E H S U N N Y N H O T A R L E
R D U M T A P E A U I W T O N
U A O M I L C O H C D F H U T
M Y R E F M E K L O Y A D D I
O S P R I N G H O L I D A Y N
P E E O Z A I M W D R D Y Q E
R A I N I N G T E N A A U P S
N H S N O W I N G R T C O M D
L O X U V A L F T T L N K S A
I N D E P E N D E N C E D A Y
```

B Look at the words in A. Write four seasons, six weather words, and six holidays and special occasions.

⊞ DO THE MATH

UNIT 1

Look at the picture. Count the items and write your answers.

1. desks   _____

2. chairs   _____

3. clocks   _____

4. boards   _____

5. books   _____

6. pens   _____

Look at the clock. What is the time now? Do the math. Write the time of each appointment.

Person	Time of appointment
1. Sonal's appointment is in four hours.	_____
2. Anna's appointment is in 30 minutes.	_____
3. David's appointment is in five hours and 30 minutes.	_____
4. Lihn's appointment is in one hour and 15 minutes.	_____
5. Eduardo's appointment is in three hours.	_____

Look at the date. Do the math. Complete the sentences.

1. Elle's birthday is March 25th. Her birthday is _____ days from now.

2. Stacey's birthday is March 14th. Her birthday is _____ days from now.

3. Santiago's birthday is March 18th. His birthday is _____ days from now.

4. Ken's birthday is March 30th. His birthday is _____ days from now.

5. Jenny's birthday is April 1st. Her birthday is _____ days from now.

UNIT 4

Look at the online bank account. Do the math. Complete the sentences.

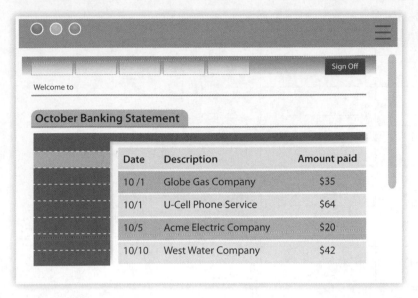

Date	Description	Amount paid
10/1	Globe Gas Company	$35
10/1	U-Cell Phone Service	$64
10/5	Acme Electric Company	$20
10/10	West Water Company	$42

1. The total for the electric bill and the phone bill is _____ .

2. The total for the gas bill and the water bill is _____ .

3. The total for all of the utility bills is _____ .

UNIT 5

Look at the map. Do the math. Complete the sentences.

How far is it?

1. It's _____ miles from San Diego to Los Angeles.

2. It's _____ miles from Los Angeles to San Jose.

3. It's _____ miles from San Jose to San Francisco.

4. It's _____ miles from San Diego to San Francisco.

UNIT 6

Look at each person's working hours. Do the math. Complete the chart.

Person	Working hours	Total hours
1. Lihn	9 a.m. to 5 p.m.	_____
2. Vidya	7 a.m. to 2 p.m.	_____
3. William	10 p.m. to 8 a.m.	_____
4. Elliot	12 p.m. to 8 p.m.	_____
5. Camilla	10:30 a.m. to 2:30 p.m.	_____
6. Emil	8:30 p.m. to 5:30 a.m.	_____

UNIT 7

Look at the receipts. How much is the change? Do the math. Write the amounts.

Save More!	***Save More!***	***Save More!***
THANK YOU	**THANK YOU**	**THANK YOU**
<<<>>>	<<<>>>	<<<>>>
Store#:006 Register #:03	Store#:006 Register #:03	Store#:006 Register #:01
Pants $20.95	Pants $15.95	Pants $23.95
Tax $ 1.68	Tax $ 1.28	Tax $ 1.92
Total $22.63	Total $17.23	Total $25.87
Cash $30.00	Cash $20.00	Cash $40.00
Change $_____	Change $_____	Change $_____
>>><<<	>>><<<	>>><<<

UNIT 8

Look at the menu. Write the price on the receipt for each item. Do the math. Write the total.

Home Cooking Coffee Shop
ORDER

Quantity	Item	Price
1	chicken sandwich	
1	vegetable soup	
1	salad	
2	cups of coffee	
	Total:	
	Thank You!	

Home Cooking Coffee Shop
MENU

Sandwiches—$6.95
Cheese and Tomato
Chicken or Beef

Soup—$3.95
Chicken and Rice
Vegetable

Salad—$4.95

Coffee or Tea—$1.50

UNIT 9

Read the medicine labels. Do the math. Complete the sentences.

1. Marisa takes _____ pills every day.

2. She takes _____ pills in total over ten days.

3. William takes _____ pills every day.

4. He takes _____ pills in total over six days.

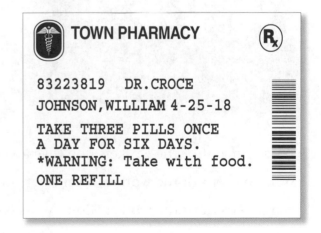

TOWN PHARMACY **Rx**

7392900   DR.FLORES
SANCHEZ,MARISA 12-08-18
TAKE TWO PILLS THREE TIMES
A DAY FOR TEN DAYS.
*WARNING: Take with food.
ONE REFILL

TOWN PHARMACY **Rx**

83223819   DR.CROCE
JOHNSON,WILLIAM 4-25-18
TAKE THREE PILLS ONCE
A DAY FOR SIX DAYS.
*WARNING: Take with food.
ONE REFILL

UNIT 10

Look at the chart about Huang's jobs. Do the math. Write the number of years Huang was in each job.

Job title	Year started	Year ended	Number of years
Childcare worker	1998	2001	1. _____
Bus driver	2002	2004	2. _____
Server	2005	2012	3. _____
Manager	2013	2017	4. _____

UNIT 11

Read about the workers. Do the math. Answer the questions.

In a small factory, there are 100 workers. Fifteen of the 100 workers don't wear safety boots. Ten of the 100 workers don't wear safety glasses.

1. What percent of the workers don't wear safety boots? _____ %

2. What percent of the workers wear safety boots? _____ %

3. What percent of the workers don't wear safety glasses? _____ %

4. What percent of the workers wear safety glasses? _____ %

UNIT 12

Read the community college catalog and the sentences about Carlos's plans.
Do the math. Complete the chart.

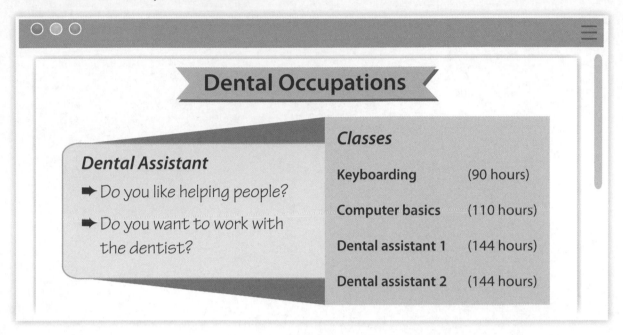

This year Carlos is going to take keyboarding and dental assistant 1. Next year,
he is going to take computer basics and dental assistant 2.

2018 Classes	Hours
Keyboarding	1. _____
Dental assistant 1	2. _____
Total hours for 2018	3. _____
2019 Classes	
Computer basics	4. _____
Dental assistant 2	5. _____
Total hours for 2019	6. _____
Total hours for 2018 and 2019	7. _____